British Railway Diesel Memories

No. 36: 'D' FOR DIESELS

D Dunn

Copyright Book Law Publications 2012
ISBN 978-1-907094-71-2

INTRODUCTION

This album has been put together to illustrate the various diesel locomotives built, ordered and operated by British Railways after the implementation of the 1955 Modernisation Plan. The classes shown cover many of the great variety of diesels run on the different regions. Presented in their different guises, are shunters and main-line diesels either working, on shed, on works or simply stabled.

It might be noticed that in a number of captions the compiler brings to the reader's attention the fact that when British Railways introduced their new crest in 1957 to replace the original 'lion and wheel' emblem, they produced one which was left facing (correct) and another which was right facing (incorrect). The ideal being that when the transfers were applied to steam locomotive tenders, the lion would always face forward, which seems logical enough to anyone. However, in Heraldry a right-facing lion is deemed to be wrong and therefore prohibited from display public or otherwise. With a double-ended diesel locomotive there was no need to have left or right facing transfers but BR supplied them to the contractors building the new diesel fleet anyway and instructions issued that the lion would face the No.1 end. Therefore, many of the new diesel locomotives which went into traffic during 1957 and 1958 carried the wrong facing transfer on the right side; that is taking the No.1 end as the front. By late 1958 the College of Heralds pointed out the faux pas to BR and reminded them it was they, the CofH, who granted the new coat of arms in the first place and therefore the application of the wrong transfers should cease immediately, and all of those already applied should be changed to the correct version with immediate effect. BR of course was somewhat chastened and vexed by the order; they had, after all, spent goodness knows how much on the new transfers and their stores were full of them! Action to stop their application at main works, and not doubt contractors too, was taken immediately but those already fixed to locomotives, steam or diesel, remained on display until the locomotive involved next went into works for a repaint. Hence a lot of diesels wore the forbidden transfers for a number of years before qualifying for a repaint. Others, such as the early withdrawals of the late 1960s, went to the breakers still sporting the wrong crest. It would be interesting to know what action the CofH would have taken, had not BR abided by the order. For those of you modelling early period diesels – that is those with a 'D' – it might be useful to know that transfers of the 'wrong facing' crest are available in various scales. However, be aware of displaying them in public!

(*Cover*) **Finsbury Park 'Deltic' D9015 TULYAR arrives at Newcastle Central with a Down express on a damp 30th August 1963.** *F.Coulton.*

(*Previous page*) **Now which one was doing all the work here? With the gradient just discernible, D286 assists? Gresley A3 No.60048 DONCASTER with a heavy and diverted southbound express along the Durham coastline at Ryhope Grange on Sunday 27th November 1960. The Type 4 was part of the Gateshead allocation and unbelievably had been in traffic for just four months when this dramatic scene was captured. The Tyneside depot certainly had something of a reputation during steam days of turning out dirty locomotives for main line express duties – it appears that the reputation was sustained with their diesel fleet. Note the use of headlamps instead of the discs. The lamps probably belonged to the A3 and were carried by the diesel for convenience, their stowage otherwise being a problem. How far the Type 4 double-headed the Pacific is not known but more than likely Northallerton would see it taken off as the ECML was regained. Note that D286 is still wearing its nose ladder (see later).** *I.S.Carr.*

Printed and bound by The Amadeus Press, Cleckheaton, West Yorkshire
First published in the United Kingdom by Book Law Publications, 382 Carlton Hill, Nottingham, NG4 1JA

Newly delivered English Electric Type 4 D200 – the class leader – stands outside Stratford's diesel multiple unit shed on Sunday 20th April 1958. The locomotive looks resplendent right down to the painted wheel rims. Everything appears as it should do except for that one mistake which was not the fault of Vulcan Foundry and was totally accredited to British Railways. That's right; the BR crest transfer has a wrong facing lion. Already by this date, BR had affixed hundreds of the new and wrong-facing crests to steam locomotives on all regions but now, in the glare of the modernisation publicity machine, it was applying the crest to the latest in BR traction! Why such a mistake was allowed to happen is a mystery given the strong wording contained in the correspondence which had already been passing between the CofH and BR for months prior to D200's appearance. Basically, the lion should face to the left – left is right, right is wrong! Without seeing the other side of the locomotive, one can only assume that a correct facing crest was applied to that particular side. Also, we are looking at the No.2 end of the Type 4 so that the crest was affixed to face the No.1 end in a rather pointless exercise of – tidiness? The other nine class members, D201 to D209, were similarly adorned but when the process was actually stopped and corrected is unknown to this compiler. D200 had arrived at Stratford depot some five weeks earlier on Friday 14th March, fresh from acceptance trials which had been carried out at Doncaster. On Tuesday 18th March it undertook a demonstration run from Liverpool Street to Norwich so, why, nearly a month after that event, the big diesel is still looking its best is something of a mystery. Perhaps it was still doing the rounds throughout the Great Eastern area? The first ten locomotives of this class D200–D209 were all put to work on the Eastern Region but it took six months before delivery from Newton-le-Willows was completed with D209 going to Hornsey in September 1958. Note the – one can only assume – headboard bracket fitted across the gangway doors, midway up the nose. It appears to be a homemade contraption slotted onto the lamp irons either side of the doorway. Note also that the Brush Type 2 on the left has no identification on its right-hand (as you see it) cab. This rather infuriating trait (as far as trainspotters were concerned!) eventually fizzled out and all of the Brush locomotives were put into traffic with 'proper' identification – with a number on each cabside. *F.W.Hampson.*

3

Another aspect of D200, alas without the BR crest in view to prove the point, outside the d.m.u. shed at Stratford on that April Sunday in 1958. It has company in the shape of Brush Type 2 D5502 which also appears quite clean considering it was delivered to Stratford in mid-December last, some four months previously. Stratford must have had some special instruction to keep their diesel fleet looking its best for as long as possible. By this date, Stratford had received about half of its first batch of twenty Brush Type 2s (D5500–D5519), the last one arriving in December 1958, just two months before the next batch from Brush was put into traffic. Although the Brush A1A-A1As became synonymous with Stratford depot and the Great Eastern lines, the ten EE Type 4s, which had set the pace of the next generation of GE line expresses, had transferred to the London Midland Region by September 1967. The glare of publicity which welcomed their coming to the Eastern was never to be theirs again. Relegation to secondary passenger services and freight work was all that beckoned from there onwards. However, it must be said that the EE Type 4 became a reliable workhorse and considering its restricted route availability, it had something of a long life on BR. D200 and her nine sisters arrived on BR without the small ladder fixed on each nose end; locomotives from D210 onwards got that fitting until it was curtailed from D324 onwards. Those ladders were somewhat short-lived and although more than a hundred of the class were so fitted, they all had them removed by 1962; tell-tale mounting screws could be seen for some years after the removals. Note the sleepered roadway crossing – concrete slabs had yet to be introduced to most BR depots. *F.W.Hampson.*

EE Type 4 D221, and a sister engine, receive attention at Longsight on 24th April 1960 surrounded by steam locomotives which are likewise undergoing repair. This is the south shed at 9A which, just a few years earlier had undergone a rebuild which took into account the future use of the premises by diesel locomotives. The original shed had twelve roads of which eight were dead-ended. It was that portion of the building covering those eight roads which was rebuilt the other four were left roofless and used for through running between the yards and for locomotive and equipment storage. At the same time the number of roads within the rebuilt shed was reduced to six, so allowing more room for fitters to work. Note also that the pits had fluorescent lighting built into the walls; I wonder how often they were cleaned? Although perhaps primitive now, the space and lighting offered greatly enhanced conditions for personnel who were more used to working in cramped, dark spaces usually with oil lamps. Apparently, steam locomotives were not allowed inside this shed until their fires were dropped! That glass roof certainly made life more pleasant but tidiness and housekeeping was still at pre-diesel days expectations with the floor used as a store for all things steam! Longsight depot was associated with the EE Type 4 from their introduction onto the LM Region until their demise from BR in the 1980s as Class 40s. *J.Archer.*

Here is a nice one for the modellers who like to weather their rolling stock. Camden based EE Type 4 D297 stands at Polmadie's refuelling pad on 6th May 1961 after working in from London with the Down *ROYAL SCOT*. Although steam power was still used for the Anglo-Scottish expresses, the EE Type 4s had begun to take the lions share of the workings and would remain the dominate type until electrification reached Euston from the north. The final nail in coffin for this class working the WCML express passenger trains came in 1967 when the D4XX class Co-Cos began to emerge from the same factory where most of these locomotives were built – Vulcan Foundry. Still, they had a good run hauling the premier expresses of their day. Memories of their deep throated growl as they approached at speed will always remain; their whistling when idling, the explosive exhaust when getting underway and accelerating. Being alongside one when it started up! Some of the first ever diesel locomotive sounds heard by this compiler were made by the EE Type 4. Even then, as a youngster, when steam was king and the diesels were the rogues, I had a soft spot for these big, heavy, noisy, ugly leviathans. Note the position of the headboard compared with where the split headcode and central headcode types carried the train name board. Also, even by this date, note the absence of the nose-end ladder. *C.J.B.Sanderson.*

Two sides of the early version of the EE Type 4. (above) Basking in the evening sun, and showing off its right side, a fairly clean D216 CAMPANIA, with No.1 end nearest, stands alongside the recently commissioned fuel tanks at Polmadie depot on 1st August 1964. Note that the Upperby based locomotive sports the correct version of the BR crest. (below) Some two years earlier, on a rather dull 28th July 1962, Edge Hill's D215 AQUITANIA stands at virtually the same location at Polmadie – albeit with the camera now pointing westwards – but is showing off its left side with No.1 end nearest the camera. The yellow warning panel was fairly new then but its effectiveness was not all that good. You could certainly hear these locomotives approaching from some distance away. It appears that somebody has made a half-hearted effort to clean this machine – they should not have bothered. both *C.J.B.Sanderson*.

Relegation to secondary and freight workings during the mid to late 60s' saw the EE Type 4s on the LMR working from depots which had hitherto hardly seen their ilk. On Sunday 9th June 1968, Allerton based D223 LANCASTRIA was recorded at Lostock Hall shed which, at that time was one of the few fully working steam depots on BR so the big diesel was lucky to have got any attention from visiting photographers. Note that the locomotive appears to have recently visited Crewe for an Intermediate overhaul – the bogies at least having some attention – whereas a full repaint was still some time in the future for the nine-years old 1-Co-Co-1. The front now has the full yellow covering but the green bodywork would suffice until the Rail blue livery was applied. From this aspect it appears that the connecting gangway doors have been welded, a feature to gladden the hearts of crews especially during the coming winter; all trace of the one-time nose ladder being fitted has also been erased; the screws removed and their holes filled. Withdrawn from Kingmoor depot in May 1981 as 40023, the Class 40 spent nearly four years rotting prior to being cut up at Crewe. *A.Ives.*

Window cleaning EE Type 4 style! D304, waiting to depart Polmadie shed to take on a southbound working in August 1962, reveals the nose roof hatches used for access to those front windows. The constant draught caused by the front gangway doors must have been exacerbated by those openings on top of the nose, so were they eventually welded up too. Note the electrification warning panel on the inside of the hatch. *David J.Dippie.*

It appears that Doncaster was proud of its 350 h.p. 0-6-0DE shunter fleet. At least that seems to be the case with D3623 seen outside the old repair shop at the south end of the engine shed on Sunday 23rd June 1963. Note the specially painted 36A shedplate adorning the front panel. Now look at the unidentified 9F 2-10-0 alongside! The Darlington built diesel was put into traffic in September 1958 at Retford whereas the last batch of the Doncaster fleet of BR Standard 9Fs arrived at 36A from Swindon works between September and December 1958; the previous March had seen another ten 9Fs arrive new from Crewe. By September 1963 the Swindon lot had dispersed to other sheds whereas the Crewe lot stayed put until early 1964 when they were laid up, withdrawn and then sold for scrap! Steam was certainly out of favour. As for this particular 0-6-0DE, it too was withdrawn in that same decade; described as 'non-standard' with a Blackstone engine and therefore surplus! Along with numerous sisters, D3623 was sold to a local scrapyard and left Doncaster shed without fanfare or even a second glance. Note that the ladder on this side of the body has been removed whilst the fixings are still fitted to the radiator housing. *C.J.B.Sanderson.*

Given Crewe's impeccable record for turning out new locomotives fairly rapidly, there must have been some supply problem with components concerning the last four of the 'Peaks' which they built. Up to D53, which was delivered in June 1962, the Works turned them out at a rate of about four units a month. Next up was D54 but that did not go into traffic until 11th August which was late, even allowing for the annual works holiday. Next in line was D55, illustrated here at a location in the works yard just west of the paint shop, with the morning sun lighting up the No.2 end on Saturday 18th August 1962. Nothing wrong with that you might think. Just a week after D54 gets to work, D55 appears ready to join in too. However, it was to be another month before D55 joined D54 at Derby. D56 kept a low profile until 24th November 1962 but the final member of the class D57 (between Crewe and Derby the numerical and chronological order became somewhat confused or at least untidy) took the prize for lagging behind with a delivery date of 22nd June 1963 – nearly one year after 'normal' delivery of the class had ceased! Never mind. Let's enjoy this pleasant picture of a brand new 'Peak' at its birthplace surrounded by steam locomotives. Finally, what did the E2 in the headcode signify – end No.2 for a painting and transfer application guide? *C.J.B.Sanderson.*

When BR decided to demolish the remaining half of the steam locomotive shed at Scarborough in the summer of 1966, the shed roads were still required for stabling visiting diesel locomotives. However, even in 1965 and long before the H&SE was 'conceived', somebody realised that falling masonry, demolition balls and diesel locomotives don't get on well together. So, to cut down line occupation and light engine mileage, certain platform roads at Scarborough's terminal station were set aside for stabling visiting diesel locomotives. On Sunday 27th June 1965 this cosy scene was captured on film and reveals two EE Type 3s, 'Peak' D127, and an unidentified Brush Type 2, all hogging the track serving platform 7. Type 3 D6740 was part of the Dairycoates allocation and could have been in Scarborough for any number of reasons, whilst the other Co-Co, D6745, was one of Tinsley's batch so would probably have worked into the resort with a weekend excursion. The Brush too was more than likely Tinsley or Wath based and would have brought an excursion from south Yorkshire or even north Derbyshire. D127 was part of the Midland Lines pool so could have arrived from any number of places with weekend revellers. So, savour this rather nice, and rare, scene from an era long, long ago! Incidentally, the straight road shed at Scarborough was actually still in use for stabling on this date (see later). *N.W.Skinner.*

Brush Type 4 D1524 made history of sorts by becoming the first of its class to visit Scarborough. On a damp Sunday 4th August 1963, and barely seven weeks after entering traffic, this Finsbury Park based locomotive managed a day at the seaside. The big diesel is stabled alongside the former 'open to the elements' coaling stage which backed onto Seamer Road. The large rectangular tank above the Co-Co supplied the depot's water requirements which, by this date, would have been rather less than the amount of previous years. However, the holiday season visits by steam locomotives continued until about 1966 and although coal was no longer available, water certainly was. D1524 would require neither, at least not today. It would be interesting to know what particular working brought this locomotive to Scarborough; was it a remnant of the *FLYER* from King's Cross or simply a holiday extra, excursion perhaps? *N.W.Skinner.*

Stabled on the same length of track as the Brush 4, alongside the coaling stage, but nearly one year later, two English Electric Type 1s have been brought to a stop a bit nearer to the old roundhouse shed which was used at that time for providing covered winter accommodation for Scarborough's small fleet of out-stationed, York based diesel shunters. We are looking roughly northwards in this view as opposed to the opposite direction in the previous illustration. The locomotives, D8066 and D8062, were part of the twenty-strong Tinsley allocation and would appear to have arrived at the head of an excursion from the Sheffield area on this Saturday, 13th June 1964. *N.W.Skinner.*

Another view of Scarborough shed yard in June 1964. Its the glorious Saturday morning of the 27th as Sulzer Type 2 D5099 complete with 50A shedplate secured to the gangway door, and Brush Type 4 D1505 – another Finsbury Park engine – are positioned ready to work over to the station for further duties. *N.W.Skinner.*

With the big uns' getting the prime stabling room inside the station, the little uns' had to go elsewhere during the weekends at Scarborough. This is the Londesborough Road carriage sidings on Sunday 25th July 1965 with one 0-6-0DE and five 0-6-0DMs – including 03 and 04 types – huddled together but in perfect frontal alignment. All of these shunters were sub-shedded from York and during the summer months would stable at this location. Winter quarters at that time consisted the old roundhouse further down the line at Seamer Road. *Both N.W.Skinner.*

One of the various NBL hydraulic designs purchased by BR was the seventy-three 225 h.p. 0-4-0DH shunters which first appeared in 1957 with gradual annual deliveries reaching into 1961. All were intended for work in the Scottish Region, at sheds which nearly all had NBR/LNER ancestry either north of the Clyde or on the eastern side of the country between Dundee and Edinburgh. D2746 emerged from NBL in February 1960 and was allocated to St Margarets where twenty other members of the class would eventually congregate. This view at Edinburgh's Waverley station on 25th July 1963 shows the little diesel performing the kind of task which they were acquired for. On 2nd November 1963 D2746 transferred to Dundee for a thirty month stint on Tayside but returned to St Margarets on 23rd April 1966. Less than a year later it was decided to move all the St Margarets diesel shunters across town to Leith Central, the former passenger station cum diesel depot, as a prelude to the 1st May closure of 64A. Thus D2746 went to its new home on the 18th February 1967 on what proved to be a short term residency; just two weeks later, on 4th March, the 0-4-0DH was withdrawn along with others of its ilk. By the summer it had been hauled down to Rotherham where many more of the class were gathered for scrapping by the Slag Reduction Co. at Ickles. Eleven of the class had actually left Scotland earlier for further duties at two railway works in England, seven to Crewe and the remainder to the carriage works at Wolverton. None lasted any longer than their counterparts north of the border and so joined the queues outside the private scrap yards. Two of the class managed to reach preservation, and those now grace two sites, appropriately in Scotland. *A.Ives.* 17

D2719 was one of the resident shunters at Crewe Locomotive Works on 16th May 1965, a job which it held down for exactly two years before the decimation of the class took place. This was one of the original batch of twelve which started work with five-figure numbers and which were some six tons lighter than the fifty-odd production models which followed. Renumbered from 11719 at Cowlairs on 20th April 1961, the little 0-4-0 carries one of the carriage-type BR crests which were applied to a lot of diesel locomotives built or overhauled during 1961. Along with the other class members which went to work at Crewe, this example too ended up feeding the steel furnaces of Rotherham. *N.W.Skinner.*

The locomotive works at Derby had long been associated with diesel locomotives. The earliest LMS attempt to create a shunting prototype was carried out at Derby in 1931. Thereafter, contractor built shunters were maintained at Derby during the 30s'. In 1939 Derby built its first 'proper' diesel shunters and continued to do so throughout W.W.II, albeit with a number of them going direct to the War Department to help with the war effort. In 1947 the first main-line diesel was built at Derby in the shape of 10000, quickly followed by 10001. From thereon, Derby was recognised as a sort of 'centre of excellence' for diesel construction and maintenance. Once the 1955 Modernisation Plan was underway, Derby took on its share of the orders for main-line diesel locomotives and produced the first of the BR/Sulzer Type 2 Bo-Bos. Next came the first of the 'Peaks' and so on. Of course the building of the vast fleet of 350 h.p. 0-6-0DE shunters carried on unabated until December 1960 when the last of them, D4010, was turned out for the Western Region. Although Derby re-organised their workshops to cater for the diesel building and maintenance – remember steam locomotive repairs were still being carried out until the mid-60s' – new facilities had to be created specifically for the diesels. One such facility was the Test House where main-line diesels underwent load testing, etc. Outside the Test House on Sunday 1st May 1966 was Type 2 D5035 – Derby built 300 of these Type 2s – which was actually one of the Crewe-built examples from August 1959, and which, at this time, was based at Willesden. It would be renumbered 24035 in April 1974 and like most of the Class 24s, would end up at Crewe from where it was withdrawn in October 1978, nearly twenty years old. Alongside is an unidentified 'Peak' which had apparently just completed a major overhaul complete with a repaint. The shedplate reveals 55A Holbeck as its home depot. All of the buildings in this illustration, along with the locomotives, are now pure history. *A.Ives.*

19

D801 VANGUARD was the second of the Swindon-built 'Warships' to be put into traffic. Emerging from works during the third week of September 1958, it was allocated to Laira depot on 7th November after extensive acceptance trials. On arrival in Plymouth it was named after the Royal Navy's last Battleship H.M.S. Vanguard which at that time was flagship of the Royal Navy Reserve Fleet based in Portsmouth harbour; the warship was decommissioned on 7th June 1960 and sailed for scrap, albeit in tow, to Faslane two months later. Swindon meantime was still delivering it's 'Warships' and had reached D825 by August 1960. D801 is seen here alongside the fuelling pad at Old Oak Common (most of the equipment was left-over from the abortive Oil fuel scheme of 1946) on Wednesday 7th October 1959. After a year in service the B-B still looks in reasonable condition. Note the Great Western style three-character train identification number frame adorning the nose, but effectively blocking the air vents, when in use. These frames were only fitted to locomotives up to D812, all subsequent class members receiving the flush fitting four-character indicator box from new. D800-D812 also later received the indicator boxes. With virtually a decade of reliable service behind it, D801 was put into store at Laira during June 1968 but just five weeks later it was withdrawn, the first of the class to go. *N.W.Skinner.*

One of the last 'Warships' to be put into traffic was D864 ZAMBESI which arrived on the Western Region in March 1962, it was initially allocated to Laira on 10th May 1962 and is seen stabled outside Old Oak Common shed on the morning of 3rd June, just three weeks later. This was the penultimate (numerically) North British Locomotive Co.–built 'Warship' to be put into traffic, it had the inset four-character headcode and the yellow warning panel; other 'Warships' visible in this illustration have either no headcode and no warning panel, or head codes but also no warning panel! This view of the massive Old Oak repair shop shows that it has basically been turned over to diesel use by now, a convenient facility which gave the diesels a modicum of the 'cleanliness' they required in their upkeep. Note the single NBL works plate mid-way along the solebar of D864. Another piece of transport nostalgia can be seen above the locomotive as a DC8 airliner peels off the 'stack' and begins its U-turn for a final line-up with one of Heathrow's runways. *N.W.Skinner.*

ENQUIRIES
SEAT & SLEEPER
RESERVATIONS

60102

The cost of equipping BR with new motive power was enormous and the great organisation was already haemorrhaging from continuous annual losses. In order to save a bob or two, redundant assets were sometimes resurrected in the most unlikely circumstances. Such was the case at Leith where the former North British Railway passenger station known as Leith Central, which had closed in April 1952, was altered to house diesel multiple units and diesel locomotives. The decision to use this place was taken in 1955 – up to that time it was used for carriage storage – and work started in 1956 to convert the two island platforms and four track layout of the place. The ex-station was conveniently located at the end of a branch, which allowed instruction of the new motive power to proceed undisturbed by depot 'comings and goings' which would have been the case at either Haymarket or St Margarets. By 30th August 1957 this is the result of the conversion with Inter-City multiple units being cared for whilst instruction in both their care and working was being carried out to all the necessary personnel drawn from all over the Scottish Region. Up to this time no diesel locomotives had yet graced the premises but that time was not far away and by the end of 1958 the big diesels started to arrive. They came and went at different periods to enable the instructors to get the most out of the classes they were teaching, be they fitters or drivers. The first type to arrive was an English Electric Type 1, on loan from the LMR in October 1958. This was closely followed by a BRC&W Type 2 (see earlier). Further EE Type 1s came in 1959 then in 1960 the really big diesels came in the shape of EE Type 4s. The final design to lend itself to the teaching staff was the BR/Sulzer Type 2 which came in 1961. Once the teaching was concluded, the place became a depot for the care and maintenance of diesel shunters and railcars. Stabled at this grandest of diesel depots on 2nd January 1969 were: Barclay 204 h.p. 0-4-0s Nos.D2413, D2415, D2416, D2417, D2418, D2419, D2426, D2443 (four of which were withdrawn); Hunslet 204 h.p. 0-6-0s Nos.D2590, D2596, D2597, D2618 (all withdrawn); BR 350 h.p. 0-6-0s Nos.D3882, D3883, D3888, D3889, and D3890. Also present were a pair of four-wheeled railbuses, SC79971, a Park Royal vehicle, and ex-Western Region based W79977, a shorter and lighter version from A.C. Cars. *C.J.B.Sanderson.*

(*opposite*) Late morning arrivals at King's Cross on Monday 27th October 1958. Details of either train are unknown but the BRC&W Type 2 is D5301, one of three of its class working from Hornsey depot at this time. A fourth member, D5303, had been delivered to Hornsey during the previous week but was en route to Inverness on this date for a two week loan to 60A, followed by a further two weeks at Eastfield, 65A, and then three weeks at Leith Central 64H, where it was used to instruct both drivers and fitters prior to the introduction of the class to Scottish Region. D5301 itself had been at Hornsey since 12th September, the second of a batch of twenty (D5300-D5319) allocated new to 34B during the delivery period July 1958 to March 1959. D5300 to D5305 all moved to Scottish Region by April 1960 whilst the other fourteen settled in at the newly constructed diesel depot at Finsbury Park on 24th April 1960. However, these Type 2s had little time left on the Great Northern main line workings and by the following October they were all transferred to Scottish Region depots. The A3, No.60102 SIR FREDERICK BANBURY was a Doncaster engine; note the wheeltapper alongside. *I.S.Carr.*

There wasn't much substance beneath that bodywork really. North British-built 0-4-0DH D2904 gets attention at Derby works on the 30th May 1965. Besides what appears to be a radiator – or cooler group – problem, the batteries are getting a charge; note the battery box cover lying on the ground. This fourteen strong class of shunters was introduced in 1958 with the first eight being delivered new to what was then acclaimed as Britain's first purpose-built diesel depot at Devons Road, in Bow. When that establishment closed its doors on 10th February 1964, the resident diesels moved across to Stratford depot. Two years later, when the work for which these 0-4-0s were designed to perform started to disappear in east London, D2904 was transferred to Wolverton carriage works on 21st May 1966. By the end of that year, on 3rd December, D2904 moved yet again; this time to Crewe. However, even though the locomotives were reliable enough – probably some of the best to come out of the NBL Co. shops – there was little work for their kind on the London Midland or any other region, BR having standardised to diesel-electric types. Of the six which never worked from Bow, four had spent much of their short lives around the Rugby and Coventry areas; the final pair being sent to Edge Hill. Weighing in at 36 tons, and with a powerful 330 h.p. engine delivering 270 h.p. at the rails, these were undoubtedly useful locomotives; the 6ft wheelbase gave them a generous route availability though the axle loading restricted them slightly. On 11th February 1967 all fourteen were condemned and later sold for scrap to Slag Reduction Co., Ickles, Rotherham who had dismantled them by the year's end. And so another shunter type became history, the late 1960s becoming a bad time for small non-standard classes, no matter how bad or good they may have been in service. *A.Ives.*

Some nice roof detail is revealed by BRC&W Type 2 D5395 in this view at Kingmoor on Saturday 16th May 1964. The filthy Bo-Bo was still allocated to the London Midland Region at this time, Leicester being its home depot, so a trip north to Carlisle would seem appropriate in the circumstances, if only to see what awaited in the not too distant future. *N.W.Skinner.*

In 1958 Swindon works built two 204 h.p. diesel-mechanical 0-6-0 shunting locomotives for Departmental use in the Civil Engineers yard at Chesterton near Cambridge – Swindon also turned-out a lot of the same for Capital Stock too. Numbered 91 and 92 in the Departmental fleet, the pair worked under that guise until July 1967 when they were taken into Capital Stock and renumbered D2370 and D2371 respectively. This is D2371 some years beforehand as No.92 at Chesterton on 1st May 1960. The view illustrates nicely the standard 0-6-0DM which became TOPS Class 03 and which was to serve BR for, in some cases, decades. This particular diesel became 03371 under TOPS and worked until withdrawn in November 1987. Somebody obviously had a soft spot for it as it was purchased privately and preserved. Note the two shunters' poles and the toe guard behind the cab footsteps. In the background the diesel's predecessor, Sentinel No.42, and an old Pullman coach appear to be getting more attention from the visiting enthusiasts than the relatively young 0-6-0DM. *N.W.Skinner.*

Although another five months were to elapse before it was finally condemned, 0-4-0DH D2700 certainly appeared incapable of any further duties in this view of 15th June 1963 at Darlington. It had arrived at works from its home shed at Goole with the coupling rods removed, as was the normal procedure when assisted travel over a long distance was encountered. However, after entry into the shops, the transmission box and final drive were removed for repair and not replaced; the locomotive being dumped 'out-of-the-way' being a sure sign that no quick turnaround was about to happen in this case. The Voith hydraulic transmission fitted to this shunter and its two sisters, D2701 and D2702, did not get on well with the Paxman diesel engine combination and all of them spent periods in store labelled 'unserviceable' but none more than the pioneer 11700, as it was first numbered when put into traffic at West Hartlepool on Monday 13th July 1953. With the BR decision to elect for a diesel-electric fleet to meet future requirements (which begs the question why also some diesel-mechanicals – 03 and others for instance), the days of fitters' struggling to keep the likes of this locomotive in traffic were over. It was finally broken-up at Darlington during November 1964; no doubt a certain amount of satisfaction went into that particular exercise. Its two younger sisters managed to struggle on into 1967 before their inevitable demise. *A.Ives.*

'Deltic' D9020 NIMBUS heads south through Durham station on Saturday 4th May 1963 with the Up *FLYING SCOTSMAN*. No headboard today but the Finsbury Park locomotive is clean(ish). This particular 'Deltic' started its working life at the London depot and finished it there too in 1980. It was the first of the class to be cut up; Doncaster, the spiritual home of the class, carrying out the deed! *A.Ives.*

Just three weeks old, Beyer, Peacock built Clayton D8598 propels an unidentified Diesel Brake Tender whilst hauling mineral empties past the long and somewhat ramshackle coaling stage of its home shed at Gateshead on Saturday 29th August 1964. At first glance, the coaling stage and the diesel seem to be in complete contrast. One looks old, tired and just about at the end of its life. The other looks new, vibrant, stylish and very contemporary, ready for anything British Railways was going to throw at it. However, as everybody knows, looks can be deceiving and as such that was virtually the case here. Without a doubt, the Clayton certainly was stylish and new but as the Scottish Region had already found out with the eighty-odd examples which they had received prior to Gateshead's lot arriving, they were thoroughly unreliable, troublesome, and not long for this world. Within four years of this event being captured on film, the first examples of the infamous Clayton class were being withdrawn, courtesy of the London Midland Region who, after a lot less than a year of their antics, wrote-off about a quarter of the class in the summer of 1968. In the meantime, D8598 and most of its sisters in the north-east continued working the kind of duties for which the class was designed – short, out and back trips, serving coal yards and lineside customers alike; note the shunters pole. But even that work was drying up. Yes, they could and were used on passenger workings but having no train heating boilers – provision had been made at the design stage to install one in the cab but they were not fitted – they were restricted to seasonal work only. A whole raft of mechanical problems had plagued the class since their introduction, many of the earlier locomotives being returned to their maker at Derby whilst complete yet undelivered examples were held back until the mechanical gremlins had supposedly been ousted. So, the neat and stylish Bo-Bos with the nice two-tone green livery were up against it in every department! Gateshead depot persevered with its members of the class and even resorted to cannibalism when an accident victim became the source of spares to keep others going. Eventually, the Scottish Region took in the final working Claytons from what was by then the Eastern Region; D8598, without its prefix was transferred to Haymarket in May 1971. Withdrawn during the following October, No.8598 was re-instated a few weeks later and was amongst the last half dozen working members of the class when withdrawn on the last day of December 1971, just seven years old which, in Clayton terms, was quite old! *A.Ives.*

Here is a nice picture of a Drewry 204 h.p. 0-6-0DM at its workplace – Darlington Locomotive Works – on Saturday afternoon, 26th June 1965. Note the complete absence of any warning stripes anywhere on D2069's bodywork but also look at the rivet detail revealed on the back end. Built at Doncaster, this neat little diesel was put into traffic at West Hartlepool on 19th September 1959. On the last day of June 1960 it transferred to Thornaby and exactly four months prior to this portrait, it was re-allocated to Darlington shed where its main duty appears to be as one of the works pilots. The eventual closure of the locomotive workshops saw D2069 move on to other duties and although still allocated to Darlington, it was housed at the diesel multiple unit depot until transferred to Gateshead. Renumbered 03069 in the TOPS scheme, this shunter found employment until December 1983 when it was withdrawn and then sold for scrap. Note that it has the correct facing BR crest. *A.Ives.*

Sticking to the Down fast of the ECML whilst en route to Heaton shed on 10th July 1961, brand-new Robert Stephenson & Hawthorn-built 0-6-0DM D2332 hurries as best it can between passenger trains at Durham station. This was another short-lived locomotive, BR withdrawing it in June 1969 from Gateshead shed. Besides Heaton, this 0-6-0 also worked from Percy Main – 8th June 1963 to 27th February 1966 – before transferring to the south side of the Tyne. Like many of the early BR casualties, D2332 was sold on to industry, this chap joining the NCB fleet at Dinnington Colliery near Worksop where it eked out a living until the coal mine closed and it was scrapped in July 1986! *A.Ives.*

Huddled together at this North Eastern Region steam stronghold, 0-6-0DMs D2326 and D2106 share the fresh air at the side of South Blyth engine shed on Sunday 22nd September 1963. The two locomotives, although very similar in appearance and profile, were not actually of the same class and had a number of both major and detail differences. This convenient weekend 'coming together' enables us to compare the two specimens. Both had the same engine type – a Gardner 8L3 producing 204 h.p. – and mechanical transmission systems – the Vulcan-Sinclair Type 23 fluid coupling with a Wilson-Drewry CA5 five-speed epicyclic gearbox, along with a Type RF11 spiral bevel reverse and final drive unit. The same diameter wheels, 3ft 7ins., were employed but there the similarity basically ended because different patterns were used, with either rounded or square profile spokes and different size balance weights. D2326 was built at Robert Stephenson & Hawthorn, Darlington, on behalf of the Drewry Car Co., and entered traffic at Tyne Dock shed on 2nd June 1961. Weighing in at 29 tons 15 cwt., the 0-6-0 produced 16,850 lb of tractive effort. The cab has overhangs on the roof with rain strips on the edges. The side window is a one-piece, non-opening pane. Likewise, the cab door window, which runs parallel with the side window, was also non-opening. The front spectacle windows have a tear-drop shape with wipers. The bonnet runs parallel with the running plate to the front radiator covering, and is topped off with a conical broad-based exhaust stack. Below the running plate the front shunters' step consist two steps whilst round-headed buffers were fitted at both ends. On 8th June 1963 D2326 was transferred to Percy Main for maintenance purposes and it was out-stationed to South Blyth. Gateshead then became responsible for its upkeep from 27th February 1966 until withdrawal on 20th August 1968. In the TOPS scheme it was designated Class 04. D2106 was a product of BR Doncaster and weighed exactly one ton and one hundredweight more than its sister; tractive effort though was somewhat lower at 15,650 lb. After initial acceptance at York, the 0-6-0DM was put into traffic at Percy Main on 20th October 1960 but moved to Blaydon just five weeks later. In common with D2326, D2106 also transferred to Percy Main on 8th June 1963, hence the sub-shedding to Blyth. Once again Gateshead took the little shunter under its wing as the facility at Percy Main closed in February 1966. Physically the cab, at the junction of the roof and side sheet, appears much smoother in transition but with a bolder rain strip. The larger side window was split to enable the rear section to open, whilst the door window although set much lower in the door, was also able to be opened downwards. The front windows were shaped to follow the profile of the bonnet which was set much higher at the cab end. The buffers note, are of the oval pattern. Finally, the exhaust makes more of a statement than the RS&H example. D2106 was classified 03 under TOPS and was renumbered 03106 in February 1974 but eighteen months later it was withdrawn and later sold for scrap. D2326 was sold to the NCB shortly after its withdrawal and served the national concern at Manvers Main Colliery until early 1976. *A.Ives.*

A frontal aspect of one of the BR Swindon-built 0-6-0DM shunters which eventually became a Class 03. This is D2020 (03020 from May 1974) standing in the shed yard at Immingham on Saturday 13th July 1963. The view allows us to see the front windows as described in the previous caption, also the wasp stripes adorning the radiator cowling. Note the axe-head balance weights and rounded spokes. The locomotive is in most respects the same as D2106 except that it has one of those exhaust stacks as worn by D2326 and known as a 'Saxa' type chimney after the salt container – traffic cone would have been a more appropriate nickname perhaps but those things hadn't really been seen much in Britain at that period. Arriving new at Immingham on 6th May 1958, D2020 was one of ten of the class which would eventually settle there to work the docks and yards on the south bank of the Humber. However, with the fall in wagon load traffic and the general world-wide shipping trend towards containerisation, D2020 was transferred to Norwich in July 1966 and it was at that depot, in December 1975, where the 0-6-0DM was eventually withdrawn. Like many of the BR shunters, it still had some useful life left in it and was sold to a private concern shortly afterwards. *C.J.B.Sanderson.*

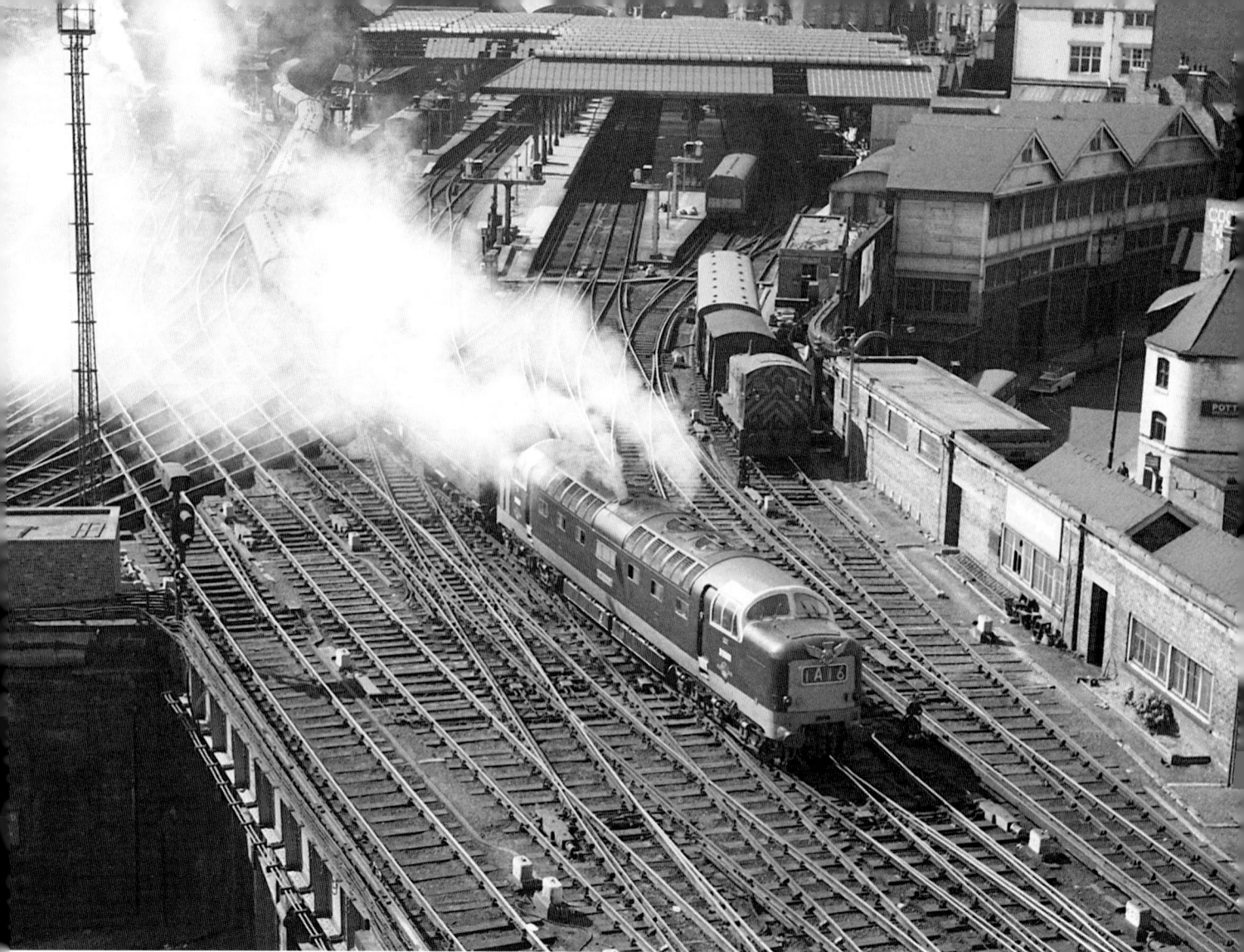

The first impression of this illustration does not bring the description 'green 'Deltic' to mind, two-tone or otherwise! In classic 'Deltic' style and with at least thirteen bogies trailing behind, Finsbury Park based 'Deltic' D9001 ST PADDY uses all of its 3,300 h.p. to ease the Down *FLYING SCOTSMAN* (1A16) over the crossing at the east end of Newcastle Central station on Saturday 29th August 1964. Note the specially cast 'flying thistle' headboard adorning the nose of the Co-Co. That particular headboard was introduced for the 'Deltic' era haulage of the famous named train but the first northbound run of the train behind a 'Deltic' took place on Monday 18th June 1962, with immaculately turned-out D9020 NIMBUS in charge. As can be seen (opposite) the usual flat-faced cast headboard with the train name *THE FLYING SCOTSMAN* was employed. *A.Ives - above, I.W.Coulson opposite.*

It has been mentioned before but the populous served by, and those working on, the railways of what is now Cumbria, or to be more precise, the railway line from Carnforth to Barrow, and then from there northwards along the coast through Workington and Whitehaven and on to Carlisle, must have had a feeling of inferiority during the mid to late 1960s when the motive power situation was given scrutiny. Metro-Vic Co-Bos and Clayton Type 1 Bo-Bos appeared to be their lot for a couple of years at least – hardly the motive power to win friends and influence people you would think. But that was a fact until the London Midland Region saw sense and tried to put matters right by withdrawing both types and drafting in the more reliable BR Sulzer Type 2s. On Saturday 15th October 1966, right in the middle of that forgettable period, two of Barrow's complement of Metro-Vic Bo-Cos, D5712 and D5714, stable at a damp Carnforth depot. Note the wrong facing BR crest adorning D5712's bodyside; that particular transfer was possibly the original specimen applied at building in Stockton, although a number of the Co-Bos did receive repaints at Crewe whilst 'working' from Barrow. As an aside, it is interesting to note that when Brush Type 2 D5500 was withdrawn and then selected for inclusion in the National Collection, it was sent to Doncaster and repainted to its original September 1957 livery specification and emerged from the works complete with a wrong facing BR crest – now you can't get more authentic than that! Should the plaudits for including that bit of historical detail go to the NRM or to somebody at Doncaster who remembered all those unusable transfers lying around a storeroom within the paint shop; I wonder if the DTG have done the same thing with their preserved Co-Bo? *A.Ives.*

Before we go any further, apologies for the out-of-focus No.2 end in this illustration. It is a Friday at the end of June 1959, it is mid-day and we are witnessing one of the North British Locomotive Co. built Type 2 diesel-electric Bo-Bos passing through Newcastle Central whilst en route to Doncaster for acceptance trials. D6120 'looks the business' and would never again appear as good as this! On 7th July 1959, with the trials and tests at 'the Plant' completed successfully, the Type 2 arrived at its new depot Ipswich. The D61XX class was one of the few diesel-electric types built by the NBL Co. and apparently they cost BR a lot of money, even before all the mechanical problems started to manifest themselves. Some thirty-eight of the class were allocated to the former Great Northern and Great Eastern lines of the Eastern Region, split initially between Hornsey (10), Stratford (10), and Ipswich (18). On 13th August 1960 – incidentally a Saturday for the superstitious amongst you – D6120 was transferred from the south-eastern corner of the Eastern Region to a point more than four-hundred miles away in Glasgow – Eastfield MPD. The ER motive power authorities had started a process during the middle of the previous April to send all of the NB Type 2s back from whence they came but it was to be 11th September before the physical transfers were completed. Apparently a big sigh of relief went around the depots and control rooms branching out from Liverpool Street but in Glasgow the cursing had only just begun. The action was actually part of a rationalisation programme whereby BR were trying to concentrate certain classes in the same area, nevertheless, it was ER's gain and ScR's loss! Our subject here was amongst those 'playing-up' and 'letting down' on a regular basis so ended up in store for much of the time. Eastfield couldn't house the scores of failures for lack of room so they were hauled near and far in order to 'clear the decks'. D6120 was condemned on the penultimate day of 1967 and was sold for scrap by the following spring. Twenty of the class escaped the mass cull of 67' and 68' simply because they had been rebuilt with new, more powerful engines and revamped electrical gear, an exercise which had made them more reliable but at what cost? The original thinking behind the rebuilding saw all fifty-eight being dealt with but a number of the class had suffered serious 'frame twisting' fires which basically wrote them off, as for the rest, common sense seems to have eventually prevailed. The twenty rebuilds were reclassified Class 29, from the original Class 21, but none of those managed to reach an age when renumbering would take place. By the end of December 1971 the last of the Bo-Bos had been condemned and none were preserved for posterity. Note the timing of those last withdrawals, coinciding with the last of the Claytons also being dealt with – Scottish Region had finally got rid of some mighty headaches. Happy Hogmanay! *David Brown.* 37

Still learning, but making do like the professionals which they were, the personnel of the Operating and Motive Power departments of the Scottish Region were in the midst of their decade-long struggle with the NBL Type 2s when this picture of D6128 was captured at Eastfield shed on 16th May 1964. The somewhat dilapidated looking diesel is not only dirty but it is stained with oil, and scratched all over the place! The Bo-Bo is located on No.5 road at the north end of the shed, in an area which appears to be dedicated to refuelling the diesels. Before it was totally rebuilt into a purpose-built diesel depot in the late 60s' Eastfield shed re-arranged the six roads on the west side of the old building to accommodate just diesels. The eventual elimination of steam enabled the rebuilding to start in earnest but that was some time off when this scene was recorded. Spotters are walking about the place filling in their notebooks (paper ones that is) whilst life at the depot carried on around them. I've mentioned this before and it is worth mentioning again – in those days I never did hear of any 'spotter' getting hurt, burnt, mutilated or killed whilst visiting an engine shed. Common sense did prevail mostly and yes there were probably a few near misses of one kind or another but we were, in the main, trusted. *A.Ives.*

Same shed, same location but from a different aspect, and at an earlier date. It is Tuesday 6th August 1963 and cleaning of diesel locomotives appears to be the order of the day! D5360, one of Eastfield's finest, gets a wash and brush-up. At this time the Glasgow depot had twenty-one of this class allocated; more were to come from the London Midland Region but those transfers did not start until 1968 when the withdrawals of the North British Type 2s started to take effect. *D.J. Dippie.*

The bleak industry scarred landscape around Wath was a legacy of the coal mining and processing which had been the principal employer in the area since the 1850s. As the country's industrial might grew so did the demand for coal and coke, the staple diet of boilers and furnaces, and the chemical by-products of its processing. West Yorkshire had more than its fair share of coal, much of it not too far below the surface, especially where the endless meadows met the Pennine barrier. However, the further east that the coalfield stretched, the deeper it got. On 9th January 1966, when this scene was recorded, many of the smaller 'pits' in the Wath area were becoming worked-out but the larger collieries just kept on churning out the coal – millions of tons of the stuff – and would continue to do so for the next twenty years or so. The large marshalling yard at Wath had been created by the Great Central Railway purely to handle the coal from those once numerous 'pits' for onward transit across the Woodhead route to Lancashire and Cheshire. Mexborough engine shed supplied the motive power for the trains taking coal from the pits to the yard at Wath. Gorton also sent their freight locomotives to Wath to help other Mexborough engines haul the coal out of Yorkshire and into Lancashire. Sixty years on and Wath yard was still in business in 1966, along with a purpose built motive power depot established to service the d.c. electric locomotives which had hauled the coal trains over the Woodhead since it was fully electrified in 1954. When Mexborough engine shed closed at the end of steam workings in the area, Wath took on a number of diesel locomotives for the pit-to-yard workings and return of the empties. Amongst the classes of diesels allocated to Wath at that time were twenty-one of the Beyer, Peacock-built Sulzer Type 2s which had been allocated new to Tinsley during 1965-66. In actuality these locomotives were sent off to Wath as they arrived from Gorton but it was April 1966 before they were all officially allocated to Wath which had its own shed code – 41C. D7635 had arrived from the makers on Bonfire Night 1965 and two months after that event it is still looking in a reasonable condition, above bogie level. This Type 2 was in the final style of the class and had been built with no gangway connections, no train heating boiler (note the empty space between the bogies where a water tank would have been fitted otherwise), a route indicator box topped the cab and either side of that are the air horns in their streamlined casings. By November 1967 the Sulzer Type 2s had been transferred from 41C, dispersed mainly to LM Region depots with a handful staying on the Eastern Region allocated to Holbeck. D7635 became 25285 under TOPS and managed a twenty year career before withdrawal in March 1986 from Crewe. *N.W.Skinner.*

Kittybrewster based NBL Type 2 D6148 takes a break at Haymarket shed on 2nd April 1961 alongside an unidentified EE Type 4. Note the discs on the NBL diesel were split top to bottom, to open side to side whereas everybody else's discs, including the English Electric classes, were split side to side to open up and down! This Type 2 had been allocated new to 61A on 18th May 1960 so was not yet a year old. With the closure of Kittybrewster shed in mid-August 1967, D6148, along with its twenty or so sisters which had been working from 61A since 1960, were transferred, on paper, to Ferryhill shed. D6148 never went to 61B as it was stored at Perth when the transfer went through. Neither did many of its brethren bother to turn up at Ferryhill either because most of them were in store, unserviceable, at places such as Elgin, Inverurie and Kittybrewster. Of course that situation could not be allowed to carry on and all the lot were condemned on the penultimate day of 1967, many being sold shortly afterwards for scrap. The Scots certainly do seem to treat the New Year as exactly that! *N.W.Skinner.*

A Portsmouth to Cardiff train pauses at Bath (Spa) station on Thursday 16th July 1964 whilst in the charge of a grotty looking Hymek, D7045 of Bristol Bath Road shed. Inter-regional and secondary passenger services, such as this, were the ideal traffic for these hydraulics. Of course freight and parcels traffic also became part of their remit, as intended from the outset. Based mainly at Bristol, Cardiff and Old Oak Common, with a few working in the West Country, the class had a somewhat slow start to their BR career when mechanical problems concerning the engines and transmission overtook them. The Western Region's response was to de-rate approximately half the class from 1740 h.p. to 1350 h.p. in the hope of finding the root cause and keeping the locomotives in traffic longer. Eventually the problems were ironed-out but it took some years with BR, the builders, engine manufacturers and the transmission makers all involved. Hindsight would perhaps say that the only good thing which came out of the all those events – which incidentally affected the other WR hydraulic classes to some extent – was a lesson in how not to do things! It is worth recollecting that five of these locomotives – the same five incidentally – worked as bankers on Lickey for five years until the LMR once more took control of the line and eventually put their own motive power on the job. *N.W.Skinner.*

Stabled in the bay at the south end of the Up island platform at Doncaster station on Tuesday 30th May 1961, 'Deltic' D9003 presents an impressive sight. The reason for this late morning 'rest' by the three-month old Co-Co is unknown but every permutation between waiting to take on a southbound working to it being a dumped 'failure' could be used. Of course within a short time this particular locomotive was to be named after one of Doncaster's famous racehorses – MELD. *I.W.Coulson.*

I'm not sure that the Designers, Makers or even the Motive Power authorities had this kind of scenario in mind for the diesel fleet during the transition period when diesel traction had to share stabling space with steam locomotives – windows and doors left open regardless whilst in close proximity of steam – but it happened regularly as highlighted here at Haymarket depot during the summer of 1963. Gateshead 'Deltic' D9014 has been left to the 'elements' with not a thought of the extra dirt which would accumulate inside the cab and engine room of the big diesel. It was one thing to teach a driver to handle another locomotive type but it was quite another to remove ingrained habits which had not before been in question – closing doors and windows! After all, steam locomotives were just left on shed, doors and windows did not really exist, especially to keep the footplate clean. Haymarket shed was still very much intact at this time, the conversion into a diesel depot had not yet got underway in earnest so keeping these expensive machines in a suitable environment for servicing and maintenance purposes was a thing for the future. Note that the large version of the BR crest sits exactly where D9014's forthcoming THE DUKE OF WELLINGTON'S REGIMENT nameplate will be fixed, resulting in two smaller emblems being used and positioned on the cab side, one beneath each number; the Deltics were the only class to carry four BR emblems although certain shunter types managed to unofficially acquire more than their quota of two when engine room panels were 'exchanged'. *C.J.B.Sanderson.*

EE Type 1s D8022 and D8026 meet stablemate EE Type 3 D6793 at Morpeth on Thursday 17th September 1970. The Bo-Bos were en route along the ECML to one of the opencast coal mines located to the north of Morpeth whilst the Co-Co has charge of a train of loaded hoppers from the Widdrington opencast coal mine which was situated just eight miles north of this junction. All three locomotives still sport their 'D' prefixes and being Gateshead engines they naturally wear heavy coats of grime. Just to the right of the signal box is the start of the branch line to Bedlington – located some four miles distant – from where access to a number of collieries, still turning out millions of tons of coal each year, was gained. Cambois diesel depot, a power station and a number of important industries were also served by that branch. *I.S.Carr.*

45

After working up from Crewe over the weekend, BR Sulzer Type 2 D5133 rests at Polmadie in the bright autumnal sunshine of Sunday morning 20th October 1963. Already three years old, the Crewe based Bo-Bo was a regular visitor to Glasgow with parcels trains and fitted freights, jobs for which they were initially designed to do. New from Derby on 24th September 1960, Longsight became its first home but not for long because two months later it was transferred to Crewe. On Christmas Eve 1960 it went to Willesden for an eighteen month stint prior to taking a one month secondment to Carlisle Canal shed! After that interlude, working the Waverley route during probably the warmest weeks of summer 1962, it returned to Longsight on 14th July. Not able to pin down the Type 2 for any length of time, 9A saw it return to Crewe on 22nd September 1962. In March 1966 D5133 was transferred to Bletchley but went back to Crewe during the following October. No matter where it roamed, the Bo-Bo always returned to Crewe and it was from there in March 1978 that D5133 – now renumbered 24133 – was withdrawn. Unlike many withdrawn diesel locomotives during that period, which spent many months and sometimes years in store, 24133 was sent to Doncaster works and cut up with seemingly indecent haste in September 1978. Did BR get their money's worth out of these Class 24s after eighteen to twenty years service? My guess is that they probably managed to break even when all the maintenance and fuel costs were included in the calculations. Did they put the mileage in? Most certainly and, added to their versatility, and reliability, they were rather good locomotives. *C.J.B.Sanderson.*

More than nineteen months since it was put into traffic at Gateshead shed on 16th November 1960, BR Sulzer Type 2 D5110 still carries that special Darlington finish to the edging of its radiator and ventilator coverings, which distinguished those 1960 Darlington-built Type 2s from the Crewe and Derby built examples. Seen at Blaydon shed on Tuesday 10th July 1962 and attached to the all important Diesel Brake Tender – the number of which is unknown – the Bo-Bo was engaged, like many of its class based at 52A, in the mineral hauling business where unfitted hopper wagons usually made up the formation of the trains. Blaydon of course was simply a stabling point for the Gateshead diesels at this time, although steam locomotives were still much in evidence as can be seen by the activity around the coaling stage. Note the 52A shedplate on D5110's connecting gangway door, smart or what? *C.J.B.Sanderson.*

By the 1st May 1966 the motive power depot at Doncaster had been basically turned over from steam to diesel maintenance and servicing. Most of the steam locomotives had been cleared out of the shed and only a few remained on the yard, put to one side to await buyers from the scrap metal business. The diesels had taken over. However, Doncaster depot never did have any main-line diesel locomotives allocated, plenty of shunters in all shapes and sizes were 'on the books' but never one of the big uns'. These three specimens basking in the Sunday afternoon sun at the north end of the shed were all from Immingham, a depot which supplied Doncaster with its daily requirements of main-line motive power for all sorts of duties. D5534 was a recent arrival at 40B from Stratford; since new in June 1959 this Brush had been allocated to former Great Eastern sheds, March (11th June 1959), Norwich (31st October 1959), Stratford (20th March 1965). Its next transfer was on 25th August 1967 when it went back to East Anglia for a spell at Ipswich. Next in line was D5593 which was soon to return from whence it came: New to Hornsey shed on 25th February 1960, it moved into the new premises at Finsbury Park at the end of the following April. In March 1961 Stratford beckoned; the swapping of these locomotives between Finsbury Park and Stratford was a regular occurrence but throughout the Eastern Region this class especially appear to have done more transfers than most during that first decade. Transferred back to Finsbury Park on 27th March 1965, D5593 re-allocated to Immingham three months later. In the July following this photographic record, it returned once again to 34G. Tucked away at the back of the line is ex-works D5567 which had a similar transfer story but with a few twists. New to Hornsey on 26th November 1959, it moved to Norwich on 16th April 1960 and managed to put in five years work solely from 32A. On 9th October 1965 it was transferred to Tinsley and went to Immingham during the following February. *A.Ives.*

Clayton D8600 heads west on a short trip to Thornaby yard in 1967 after passing through Middlesbrough station with a train of finished steel from Lackenby. This is the kind of work the Clayton Bo-Bo was designed for. Note the shunters' pole balanced on the bufferbeam – pure North Eastern. *A.R.Thompson.*

This is a section of the western (no pun intended) side of 'A' shop at Swindon on Saturday 7th October 1961 with three 'Western' class diesel-hydraulics being built. The only one easily identifiable is D1002 – a.k.a. No.3 – on the left of the trio. Apparently D1001 stands on the right, whereas D1000, as yet to be named WESTERN ENTERPRISE, has centre stage. All three diesels are still some way to completion and fitters can be seen attending to them all. The class leader did not emerge from works until December; D1001 was some time behind and was not allocated to Laira until 24th February 1962! However, just a month behind that was D1002. Thereafter, Swindon started to turn out the 'Westerns' at the rate of one a month; Crewe managed two! Note the somewhat substantial engine/transmission/gearbox couplings on the floor in front of D1002. *N.W.Skinner.*

(*opposite*) To say that the Western Region was disappointed with their five North British A1A-A1A Type 4s would be something of an understatement. To say that British Railways were disappointed with the Western Region would be another gross understatement. However, somebody had to go down the diesel-hydraulic road and the WR, being the WR, chose that particular path with the total backing of the British Transport Commission it may be added. If the British taxpayer had been made fully aware of the waste taking place there might have been some serious scalp collecting. As it was, nobody was brought to book and perhaps worst of all, those responsible still thought they were doing the right thing even when it was plain to everybody else that things had gone seriously and expensively pear-shaped. It might be said that the five original 'Warships' of the D6XX series were thrust upon the WR by the BTC with political, economic, and some self-interest, being the main contenders for ordering them in the first instance. Thirty-three more of the big 117 ton machines had been an optional order but in the event NBL Co. converted the option to thirty-three of the lighter weight D8XX B-B locomotives. D601 ARK ROYAL arrived at Swindon from its makers in Glasgow on 24th March 1958 and in this three-quarter view from 1st June 1958 it was still undergoing testing of sorts. On the 14th of that month it was released from Swindon and sent to its designated home at Plymouth Laira where D600 had also just arrived after its prolonged trials at Swindon. The next two members of the class did not appear from NBL until the following November by which time the two early birds had become regular and reliable haulage for the West of England express passenger services. And that is when it all started going wrong. The fifth and final member of the class arrived in January 1959, exactly a year after D600's arrival at Swindon. The three 'late arrivals' started to give trouble from the moment they reached Laira depot; the initial pair were still working the expresses but their performance too was declining. The 2,000 h.p. and the heavy weight of the locomotives themselves was not a good combination. Laira struggled to achieve the mileages which had been designated to these hydraulics but components large and small, mainly the latter, were failing continuously. D601, along with D602 and D604 were transferred to Landore in August 1967 in a last ditch attempt to see if anyone could find something useful about this class. The attempt was a failure and by the end of November the trio had returned to Devon. Salvation came on the following 30th December when all five were condemned and then sold for scrap! *C.J.B.Sanderson.*

BR Sulzer Type 2 D5181 runs the Consett-Tyne Dock iron ore empties over the road crossing at Biddick Lane on 18th July 1966. Steam had by now been totally eliminated from haulage of the iron ore trains and these successful Bo-Bos were found to be the best available motive power for a somewhat awkward and taxing working. Various diesel classes had been tried on the iron ore workings; perhaps the most exotic were a pair of Clayton Type 1s which arrived from Polmadie on loan to Tyne Dock shed on 5th September 1963 and for the next week were tried both singly and in multiple on the arduous ascent to Consett steel works. Afterwards the pair went south to Ardsley but nothing came from the September 1963 trials because when the North Eastern Region got their quota of Claytons from the Beyer, Peacock batch, none were apparently used on the Tyne Dock ore trains. *I.S.Carr.*

Before the diesel multiple unit shed at Sheffield Darnall was altered for main line diesel use, the resident diesels at Darnall were quite happy to rub shoulders with the resident steam locomotives. This view of 350 h.p. 0-6-0DE D4090, outside the western end of the steam shed on 29th April 1962 shows the aforementioned d.m.u. shed in the background. That shed was, by this date, fully functioning as a diesel depot but such were the numbers of diesel locomotives allocated to 41A, it was necessary to still use the somewhat spartan facilities offered by the steam shed – Grimesthorpe depot had been and was still being used for stabling some members of the 41A diesel fleet at this time. When the purpose built depot at Tinsley was eventually commissioned in April 1964, a mass exodus of diesels took place but a small batch of these 350 h.p. shunters remained behind at Darnall and actually moved in with the d.m.us in their own shed. The nicely turned-out shunter wears the green livery of the day along with wasp stripes at both ends and of course the lettering and figures of the numbers which were described as 'Condensed Grotesque' with serifs added to the D to make it stand out more than the original sans serif style of D. D4090 was a only weeks old when this scene was captured. Turned out new from Darlington, it was first allocated to Doncaster but within three days it had moved to Gorton. After just five weeks at 9G, it moved back across the Woodhead route to Darnall on 27th April 1962 and posed for the photographer on the following Sunday outside its new home. This particular shunter was one of those which stayed behind in April 1964 but eventually moved to the Tinsley allocation on 9th October 1965. *C.J.B.Sanderson.*

In the summer of 1966 a start was made on equipping BRC&W Type 2s (later Class 26) on the Scottish Region to enable them to work permanently coupled trains of hopper wagons directly from coal mines to power stations without any intermediate marshalling en route. D5303 became the first of the class to be fitted out with the equipment for the soon to be introduced Merry-Go-Round (MGR) coal trains in Scotland. Slow speed control (SSC) and air braking were requirements for hauling the new air-braked hopper wagons (HAA), whilst the SSC enabled the locomotives to manoeuvre the complete trains – usually made up to about thirty HAA wagons of 33-tons each – beneath the loading silos at the mines and over the discharge hoppers at the power stations. Eventually more than twenty of the class were equipped for the MGR workings. St Rollox works carried out the conversion on the Haymarket based diesels but other BR workshops, mainly Crewe and Derby were responsible for fitting the same type of equipment into hundreds of other locomotives (mainly EE Type 1s and Brush Type 4s) of what was to become Class 20 and Class 47. External differences between D5303 and the rest of the class included having the corridor connections at each end removed and the doors welded-up, and two external cylindrical air tanks fitted in place of the heating water tank – the internal heating boiler was also removed. By July 1967 St Rollox had completed Nos. D5301 to D5307, enough to begin the workings which would initially supply Cockenzie power station from the Longannet mine. Here at Haymarket depot in early 1964, D5300 and D5306 are coupled in multiple but are yet some years away from the aforementioned conversion work prior to the MGR services. However, it appears that D5300 has already been prepared with one of its gangway doors looking very unoriginal! One of the nice touches with these BRC&W-built locomotives was the cab door handles which were placed at a sensible position, enabling crewmen to open the doors prior to climbing the steps from the ballast. *C.J.B.Sanderson.*

Brand new Beyer, Peacock Hymek D7049 rests at Old Oak Common on Sunday 7th October 1962 in the company of classmate D7036 which was visiting from Cardiff. Delivered to Bath Road depot two days previously, the immaculate B-B had probably just made its maiden revenue-earning trip from Bristol to London over the weekend. Initially rated at 1,700 h.p., approximately half the members of this 101 strong class had their Bristol-Siddeley/Maybach engines de-rated to 1,350 h.p. by the end of 1963; basically all those with odd numbers being chosen for the exercise. The 1967 decision by British Railways to standardise with diesel-electric motive power saw this class, along with all of the Western Region's fleets of diesel-hydraulics, given a death knell, the sentence of which was to be carried out by the end of 1973. D7049 complied with the order and was withdrawn in January 1972 whilst part of the Old Oak Common allocation. D7036 went six months later but the last members of the class to succumb remained in traffic, and working from 81A – OC to give the depot its 1973 code – until March 1975. *C.J.B.Sanderson.*

Now, let's try this one first. One of Motherwell's senior fitters glances at Clayton D8547 which is lined-up with others outside the depot on Saturday 16th May 1964. Obviously, the former steam shed managed to cope with the Claytons thrust upon them – all of 66B's resident Class 17s were allocated to Polmadie – but they must have been counting the days between every unscheduled repair, wondering what the next breakdown would reveal. Besides Polmadie and Haymarket, Motherwell had the next largest complement of the class working its duties. *A.Ives.*

On Monday 19th August 1963, Hymek D7010 stands at Malvern (Link) station with a Paddington to Hereford via Worcester express. This was the type of traffic suited by the class and it was on such services from London to Hereford where the last Hymek's worked prior to their withdrawal in 1975. Nowadays HSTs perform on these workings, and no doubt multiple units will continue into the future, locomotive haulage like this being consigned to history. *A.Ives.*

Another depot which had a complement of Clayton Type 1s, before they were banished to Scotland during April and May 1966, was Staveley Barrow Hill which had thirteen of the class on the books prior to the Eastern Region (shades of the NBL D61XX episode here perhaps?) managing to convince higher authority that the Bo-Bos couldn't cope with the increasing tonnage of the mineral traffic over some of the colliery lines served by the north Midlands depot. Barrow Hill already had a number of the EE Type 1s allocated, with new examples arriving regularly, and required even more to replace the Claytons. During May and June 1966 D8128 to D8133 were transferred in, ex Tinsley and only weeks old. Alongside the Type 1s, Tinsley also sent nine BR Sulzer Type 2s – D7600-D7608 – as direct replacements for the Claytons. This is D8132 stabled at the side of the roundhouse shed on 1st May 1966 with D8133 behind. One of the 'about to depart' Claytons (buffers only visible) is at the front end. This 1966-built batch of the ever reliable English Electric workhorse now carried the four-character route indicator boxes at both ends, the disc system fitted to earlier models having been discarded for this batch. Otherwise, no other changes had taken place to the design. By the end of the year the Sulzer Type 2s had re-allocated to Haymarket, swapped for a similar number of EE Type 1s! *A.Ives.*

Delivered to BR at Eastfield on 12th September 1961 (along with D8083), EE Type 1 D8084 was one of forty-six of the class allocated to the north Glasgow depot between June 1961 and February 1962. All of that batch (D8070–D8115) were built at the Robert Stephenson & Hawthorn plant in Darlington and were quickly followed by another dozen (D8116–D8127) which went to Polmadie. All of the Scottish Region examples had the inset provided in the cab side ready for tablet-catching equipment to be fitted; in the event only a few of the class, those allocated to Kittybrewster for instance, were actually fitted with the equipment. These 1961/62 RS&H deliveries were intended to be the last of the class but nearly four years after had D8127 arrived at Polmadie, D8128 was delivered to BR in January 1966 as part of an order for 100 further English Electric Type 1s which were built to replace the somewhat unreliable and disappointing Clayton Type 1s which, on their introduction in 1962, BR had pinned their 'Standard Type 1' banner to! Note the carriage style BR rounded crest adorning D8084 in place of the more usual style applied to locomotives; most of the RS&H batch had this type of crest affixed, much like the 'Western' class and some of the smaller shunters, but the 1966 Vulcan Foundry built Type 1s reverted to the normal crest. *A.Ives.*

D8086 and D8123 share a quiet moment at Polmadie on Sunday 20th October 1963. D8086 was originally allocated to Eastfield but was transferred to Polmadie on 29th September 1962. The transfer would otherwise have gone unnoticed, 65A and 66A often exchanging locomotives of this class, except that this particular Bo-Bo had just come out of works after being fitted with train air braking equipment – the two extra hoses associated with the extra fitting can be seen affixed to the top half of the bufferbeam – to enable it, and similarly fitted sister D8085 (see also later) to work empty electric multiple unit stock between the e.m.u. depots at Hyndland and Shields Road. D8085 had actually preceded its sister out of works and on to Polmadie by a couple of weeks. *C.J.B.Sanderson.*

A superb but undated view of a late running Down Anglo-Scottish, overnight, express running through Hilton Junction near Perth with BRC&W Type 2 D5321 leading EE Type 4 D304. *P.J.Robinson.*

Straight out of the box and yet to do any test runs. BR Sulzer Type 2 D7592 stands outside the shops at Darlington on Saturday 9th May 1964 having just emerged into the daylight for the first time. By now Darlington was getting towards the end of its illustrious locomotive building career; indeed the total closure of the workshops had long been announced but quality nevertheless still reigned at the North Road works. Put into traffic at Toton exactly one week after this event was recorded, the Bo-Bo was amongst the last batch of twenty to be built at Darlington. D7597, which emerged in August had the honour of being the last locomotive built at the works. Alongside can be glimpsed one of the dwindling band of Gresley Pacifics which were still being overhauled at North Road, the only workshop on British Railways still carrying out such work. *A.Ives.*

Running under clear signals, and a blue sky, Gateshead based EE Type 3 D6788 heads north through Durham station on Saturday 23rd February 1963 whilst hauling a Diesel Brake Tender and propelling a brakevan. Evidence of the severe and prolonged winter still furnishes the landscape with a layer of snow. The sun may be out but that mini-thaw would not last long; temperatures and visibility were about to drop again. The Co-Co was probably heading home for a weekend break, the continuous journeys performed by D6788 and its ilk, between the coal mines and the waiting consumers, would be on hold now until the following Monday. *A.Ives.*

The diesel depot at Bradford Hammerton Street had been fashioned from the former Great Northern engine shed after the place had closed to steam locomotives on 12th January 1958. Unlike some other establishments where diesels found a new home in refurbished old buildings, Hammerton Street remained much the same as it had done during steam days as witness this view inside the old two-road repair shop on 26th March 1966. Except for the motive power nothing had changed; the overhead crane was still chain driven and was probably never used by the diesel fitters if it was as awkward then as it had been during steam days! No elevated platforms had been built nor lighting installed in the pits. The running shed attached to the south wall of this building was mainly a parking plot for diesel multiple units whilst the reasonably-sized fleet of allocated diesel shunters – all 0-6-0s but of the electric and mechanical persuasions – would only come home for maintenance, and fuel. Cleaning, note, was not one of the normal routines carried out at the depot. *A.Ives.*

Locally built Barclay 204 h.p. 0-4-0DM D2428 stands over the ashpit at Greenock Ladyburn engine shed on Sunday 17th May 1964. Already five years old, the little shunter is looking quite smart and was one of five of the class allocated to 66D at this time – D2425, D2426, D2427, and D2429 being the others – but not for much longer as a transfer to Hamilton was less than a month away. Entering traffic on 21st December 1959 at Motherwell, D2428 spent its whole life working from sheds in Glasgow's 66 district. On 19th March 1960 it moved from 66B to Polmadie and it was from there on 25th February 1961 that the 0-4-0 transferred to Greenock. The re-allocation to 66C took place during week ending 13th June 1964. Finally on 18th May 1968 it went back to Polmadie but only briefly because on 15th June 1968 it was withdrawn, a victim of the downturn and loss of freight traffic. The class had been built specifically to work in Scottish Region and were equipped not just for shunting yards with tight radius tracks, but also for trip working hence the fitting of a vacuum ejector for train braking. Useful locomotives, they weighed in at a hefty 37 tons! Of the original thirty-five shunters comprising the class, ten managed to survive to become Class 06 under the TOPS scheme, another skipped the country for a new life in Italy. A lone example D2420 (06003, later Departmental 97804) survives to this day and is preserved at the Manchester Museum of Science & Industry. *A.Ives.*

Staying in Scotland, we have this rather nice view of EE Type 1 D8075 at St Rollox engine shed on Friday 4th August 1961, shortly after its arrival from the makers at Darlington. Coupled here to D8076 – they tended to arrive in pairs from RS&H – the Bo-Bo and its sister would have been undergoing acceptance trials together since arrival in Glasgow on 26th July, and then working from St Rollox shed under the direction of the nearby locomotive works of the same name. A nice amount of detail is on show with just a little bit of road dirt on the lower body and bogies. Both locomotives were allocated to Eastfield shed and would make their way there over within the next couple of days, assuming all was well. *David J.Dippie.*

350 h.p. 0-6-0DE shunter No.13007 rubs shoulders with the heathen steam at Eastfield shed on 8th September 1956, shortly after a major overhaul, it's first since being delivered new to Hurlford shed at the beginning of December 1952. Having just missed out on getting its 'D' prefix by a matter of months, the shunter would have to wait until 26th November 1960 before finally becoming D3007. On 5th November 1966 D3007 was transferred away from Scottish Region and started a new life at Lostock Hall where it managed to see out the last of BR steam. Renumbered 08003 under the TOPS scheme in February 1974, it was finally withdrawn at Darlington depot in December 1977 – during that last year it had already been withdrawn once but was re-instated for a few months – and then went back to Scotland to be broken up at Glasgow Works. Note the twin ladder arrangement at the front end with one each side of the radiator housing. Later models had just one ladder, usually on the left side, but they were removed completely from 1963 onwards. *C.J.B.Sanderson.*

Having got rid of its own batch of Hunslet 204 h.p. 0-6-0DMs to all and sundry by January 1964, Wakefield engine shed provided shelter for some of the Ardsley allocated machines stuck on the wrong side of the town at weekends. On Saturday 3rd April 1965, Ardsley's D2608, a rather grotty member of the 56B fleet, was captured on film stabled outside the stores entrance at Wakefield shed. Not quite five years old, D2608 was one of six Hunslet shunters (D2603-D2608) sent new to Ardsley at the end of 1960, our subject arriving there on 9th December. Three others, all second-hand, had preceded them during the previous summer. More examples, albeit second-hand too, followed, including some of the original 56A batch. However, Ardsley shed was not long for this world and on 16th October 1965 all of the 56B shunters were transferred to Hammerton Street in Bradford for a life of uncertainty. Many, including D2608, were fobbed off to Scotland in 1967, a prelude to their withdrawal later in the year. *A.Ives.*

Besides those sent to work on the North Eastern Region starting on Bonfire Night 1959 (D2586 onwards), Hunslet provided an earlier batch to the Scottish Region starting with D2574 to Stranraer, and including D2578 which was one of ten (D2576-D2585) delivered to Thornton Junction engine shed. D2578 arrived on 22nd November 1958 and its aim in life was to work the marshalling yard at Thornton and perform local trip working along with its classmates. On 7th July 1967 the 0-6-0DM was withdrawn simply because it was 'non-standard'. However, its makers Hunslet purchased it back from British Railways, rebuilt it to a customer order, and in 1968 it began a new life working for Bulmers at Hereford. Named CIDER QUEEN, D2578 worked for the private concern longer than it did for BR and at its retirement it even managed to be chosen for preservation and is active now at a site not too far from Hereford. Note that the vacuum pipe assembly is fitted to the right of the front coupling whereas on D2608 and those of the later NE Region batch, had the pipework positioned to the left of the coupling hook. *N.W.Skinner.*

Now this 0-6-0DE shunter should not, strictly speaking, be included in this album because it never did carry the 'D' prefix but it qualifies inclusion for two reasons – lots really including the compilers' tastes – one is the apparent early form of front-end warning stripes applied to the radiator covers which at this time appears to be serving no purpose whatsoever. For the record, the location is the siding adjacent to the south-west point of the New England engine shed triangle, just south of the fitting shop. The date is 1st May 1960 and the locomotive is the former LNER/Brush model which should have become No.8004, following on from the four 0-6-0DE shunters number 8000 to 8003 in the LNER series. As things turned out, our subject, had been built at Doncaster in 1946 but had not received its internal workings until sent to Brush at Loughborough in 1947, did not enter revenue service with the LNER and it was left to BR who put it into traffic at March shed as No.15004 in April 1949. It was on trial at Hornsey shed over the Christmas period of 1951 but returned to March in January 1952. Five years later it was sent to Woodford Halse in early January 1957 but ended up at New England on the 26th of that month and decided to stay! Withdrawn on 5th October 1962, it was cut up at Doncaster during the following May. Now, that second reason, which is simply an observation rather than a critique; note the gauge at the top of the radiator housing – what was that all about and who was supposed to read it!!?? Note the two sets of couplings and two shunters poles. As for the lifting brackets, Doncaster didn't pussyfoot around that problem. *N.W.Skinner.*

ACCIDENTS & INCIDENTS!!

Type 1 D8085 in dire straits at St Rollox shed on Saturday 7th October 1961, just nineteen days after delivery from English Electric; the where, and when of the incident which buckled the Bo-Bo is unknown. This is one of the Robert Stephenson & Hawthorn examples built in Darlington which have already been illustrated in this album; note the BR coaching stock emblem in place of the normal crest. Along with sister D8086, D8085 was the other Type 1 specially fitted with train air brake equipment in September 1962 to enable the pair to haul empty electric multiple unit stock between depots. Obviously, the catastrophe which befell the Bo-Bo must have been fixable (although it doesn't appear so from this angle) because it was eventually put into traffic at a later and unknown date but how much later and, at what cost? We are reliably informed that the damage illustrated was typical of a slow speed impact against another buffer fitted train, pushing the draw gear in and forcing the frame down! There had probably been some red faces but nothing relating to the incident has appeared in print, this illustration being the only known record. *C.J.B.Sanderson.*

Being adjacent to St Rollox locomotive works, the engine shed at St Rollox (Balornock) became something of a dumping ground for clapped-out locomotives during the Sixties' as witnessed this pair of NBL Type 2s dumped on a siding to the north of the shed yard on 28th July 1962. What was ailing D6114 is unknown but D6136's problem, or part of it, is easy to spot – fire damage, cause unknown. The list of ailments affecting this class was as long as a spendaholics bank statement and no matter how much effort was put into getting the Bo-Bos to work correctly, they just would not perform. Scottish Region engineers must have felt aggrieved by their lot (the additional problems which beset the Clayton Type 1s possibly introduced symptoms of paranoia amongst the motive power department), coupled with the fact that these Type 2s were built locally must have also knocked the wind out of many involved with their maintenance and running. D6114 was one of the twenty which were refurbished and fitted with a Paxman engine in 1966 but D6136 was one of those left untouched and became a victim of the December 1967 cull which effectively wiped out half of the class. Note the basic, no frills, no streamlined curves, brake tender on the right with Gresley coach bogies; was this one of the prototypes constructed by Cowlairs round about this time? *C.J.B.Sanderson.*